D0908349

Angels

Angels

A BOOK OF POEMS

by

Joan Walsh Anglund

Random House
New York

Library of Congress Cataloging-in-Publication Data
Anglund, Joan Walsh.
Angels : a book of poems / by Joan Walsh Anglund.
— 1st ed.
p.   cm.
ISBN 0-679-40903-2
1. Angels—Poetry.   I. Title.
PS3551.N47A8   1995
811'.54—dc20   95-6309

Manufactured in the United States of America
on acid free paper.
2 4 6 8 9 7 5 3
First Edition

In loving memory of my dear friend

Connie Cohen

Angels

Angels
   are among us,

. . . can you
      see them?

When God created
                the world
                            and its peoples,

He laughed,
        with pure Joy!

And
        His laughter
                        scattered

. . . and that's
            how angels
                        were born!

I thought
      I was alone

within
      a place of fear
           and darkness

. . . until I heard
      my angel
        whisper,
           ". . . I am here!"

The work
of angels
is kindness

. . . their gift to us
is Peace.

Like silver bells
          ringing
                    across the sky

is the song
          of angels!
                    . . . Listen!

It is the angels'
        delight
                to give,

as it is our
      delight
            to receive
                  of them.

The angels cry
       when
             we are cruel,

they sigh
         when we are lonely

. . . but they laugh
             when we love one another!

With your heart's deepest hope
    ... reach for your angels!

... Your believing
    brings them to you!

We must first believe
    or they cannot come to us!

As we invite them
    ... they soon attend.

Angels
    are God's
        bright messengers
           . . . of Hope!

Angels.

. . . What other name
                    would you give

these heavenly beings

. . . these joyful visitors
                    from God,

. . . except
          the name
                    of Love?

You are not alone.

. . . An angel
            is beside you

    in all
            your endeavors.

Love
    is the home

where angels abide

When troubles come,
the strongest help
is
sometimes
a
whispered prayer,
for God hears,
and sends His angels
in
answer,
to
comfort,
and protect.

The angels
  play
    at miracles.

. . . That which is impossible,
          the angels do!

We are nearest
            the angels

when we Love.

Angels
    are the
        unseen friends

who walk
        beside us

. . . while we are absent
        from our Home.

As seraphim
　　　　on high

Let us
　　　keep always
　　　　　　a joyful heart,

　　　. . . ever eager
　　　　　　to serve,

for the angels
　　　　do not sigh,
　　　　　　　. . . they sing!

And thus
　　　　with glad hearts
　　　　　　　accomplish
　　　　　　　　　great wonders!

Your angels
          are nearer
                    than you know!

Though,
        at times,
the way
        seems dark
                ahead,
God's angels
        shall safely
                lead us,
until
    we once more
                glimpse
                    the
                        Light.

Who is so strong
        that he does not need
                the kindness of angels?

Who is so wise
        that he does not need
                their guidance?

Trust your angels

        . . . they shall

                never fail you.

Do you doubt the sun?
. . . the rising of the moon?
. . . the twinkling of the stars above?

Why doubt you, then,
        the angels,
. . . whose Light is brighter
        than all these
. . . and lasts
        throughout eternity!

Angels
    are
        pure Joy!
           . . . pure Light!

. . . pure Love!

We are always safe
     . . . wherever we may go,
for unseen hands,
     the blessed touch of angels,
lead us
     ever
          toward our Truth.

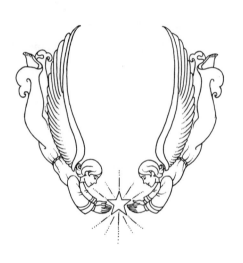

And
    when this brief life
        has ended,

. . . the angels
      shall lift us

      on golden wings,
        . . . into the Light
            from which we came.

.

About the Author

JOAN WALSH ANGLUND the much-loved author/illustrator of such celebrated titles as *A Friend Is Someone Who Likes You* and *Love Is a Special Way of Feeling*, lives with her family in an eighteenth-century house in Connecticut.

Mrs. Anglund was honored by the Lincoln Academy of Illinois for her contribution to literature and art. Her books, which have sold more than forty million copies, have been widely published all around the world in over fourteen languages.